IT'S TIME TO EAT LIMA BEANS

It's Time to Eat
LIMA BEANS

Walter the Educator

Silent King Books
A WhichHead Entertainment Imprint

Disclaimer

This book is a literary work; the story is not about specific persons, locations, situations, and/or circumstances unless mentioned in a historical context. Any resemblance to real persons, locations, situations, and/or circumstances is coincidental. This book is for entertainment and informational purposes only. The author and publisher offer this information without warranties expressed or implied. No matter the grounds, neither the author nor the publisher will be accountable for any losses, injuries, or other damages caused by the reader's use of this book. The use of this book acknowledges an understanding and acceptance of this disclaimer.

It's Time to Eat LIMA BEANS is a collectible early learning book by Walter the Educator suitable for all ages belonging to Walter the Educator's Time to Eat Book Series. Collect more books at WaltertheEducator.com

USE THE EXTRA SPACE TO TAKE NOTES AND DOCUMENT YOUR MEMORIES

LIMA BEANS

The clock says it's dinner time,

It's Time to Eat

Lima
Beans

A plate of beans is just sublime.

Lima beans, so smooth and green,

The prettiest beans you've ever seen!

They grew beneath the summer sun,

A garden gift for everyone.

Round and flat, they bring delight,

Ready to eat, they look just right.

Cook them soft, or keep them firm,

A tasty treat with every turn.

Butter melts to make them shine,

A yummy dish that's oh-so fine!

Lima beans love friends, you see,

With rice or ham, they'll always be.

Cornbread joins the tasty crew,

Dinner's here for me and you!

It's Time to Eat

Lima Beans

They're full of strength to help you grow,

From head to toe, they let it show

Jump and skip, then run around,

Lima beans keep you safe and sound!

Add a pinch of salt and spice,

Lima beans are oh-so nice.

Garlic, herbs, or just plain too,

There's no wrong way to enjoy the stew!

These beans are from a farmer's hand,

Grown with care across the land.

Harvest time, they're picked with pride,

Now they're here to be enjoyed inside!

Big and bold or baby small,

Lima beans, we love them all

Creamy bites that melt away,

Making magic every day.

So let's sit down and grab a spoon,

Lima beans are ready soon!

Take a bite, enjoy the fun,

Dinnertime has just begun.

It's Time to Eat

Lima

Beans

With every bite, our smiles grow,

Lima beans, we love you so!

Thank you, beans, for being great,

It's Time to Eat

Lima

Beans

We'll eat you all, there's no debate!

ABOUT THE CREATOR

Walter the Educator is one of the pseudonyms for Walter Anderson. Formally educated in Chemistry, Business, and Education, he is an educator, an author, a diverse entrepreneur, and he is the son of a disabled war veteran. "Walter the Educator" shares his time between educating and creating. He holds interests and owns several creative projects that entertain, enlighten, enhance, and educate, hoping to inspire and motivate you. Follow, find new works, and stay up to date with Walter the Educator™

at WaltertheEducator.com

9 798330 590520